SCIENCE
PROJECTS

FORCES AND MOTION

Simon de Pinna

Photography by
Chris Fairclough

RAINTREE
STECK-VAUGHN
PUBLISHERS

A Harcourt Company

Austin   New York
www.raintreesteckvaughn.com

Library of Congress Cataloging-in-Publication Data
de Pinna, Simon.
Forces and motion / Simon de Pinna.
      p.   cm.—(Science projects)
      Includes bibliographical references and index.
      Summary: Explains the concepts of force and motion through experiments which can be performed at home.
      ISBN 0-8172-4962-1
      1. Force and energy—Juvenile literature.
      2. Motion—Juvenile literature.
      [1. Force and energy—Experiments. 2. Motion—Experiments 3. Experiments.]
      I. Fairclough, Chris, ill. II. Title. III. Series: Science projects.
      QC73.4.P56   1998
      531'.6—dc21   97-33987

Printed in Italy. Bound in the United States.
   3 4 5 6 7 8 9 0 02 01

Picture acknowledgments
The publishers would like to thank the following for permission to reproduce their pictures:
Bruce Coleman: pages 33 (Peter Terry), 36 (Erwin and Peggy Bauer); **Ford UK:** page 22; **NASA:** page 40; **Science Photo Library:** cover (James Stevenson) and page 6; **Tony Stone Images:** pages 4 (Ken Biggs), 9 (George Lepp), 10 (Richard Kaylin), 12 (David Young Wolff), 14 (Lori Adamski Peek), 16 (Nicholas Pinturas), 24 (Janet Gill), 26 (Andrea Booher), 30, 34 (Amwell), 38, 42 (Roger Labrosse), 44 (Peter Newton).
Illustrations: Mick Gillah; Cover and page 19 Julian Baker

CONTENTS

FORCES EVERYWHERE

What are forces? Forces can launch rockets into space and split the earth apart in an earthquake. They can slow objects down, speed them up, or change the direction in which they are moving. Forces can even change the shape of an object. If there were no forces, nothing would ever happen. But sometimes forces seem to be doing nothing at all: this could be because the effect of one force is balanced by the effect of another, like two people at either end of a seesaw.

Forces cannot be seen, but you experience their effects all the time. Your weight is a force: for example, when you get out of bed in the morning, your weight pulls you toward the floor. Sit at the top of a slide and the force of gravity will pull you down. You don't move far beyond the end of the slide because the force of friction slows you down when you hit the ground.

DID YOU KNOW?

The great forces at work during earthquakes are recorded using two scales. The 12-point Mercalli scale is based on what is seen and felt during an earthquake, and ranges from "can be recorded but not felt" to "total destruction." The Richter scale is a 10-point scale that measures the energy in a tremor. The strongest earthquake ever occurred in Tokyo, Japan, in 1923, and measured just under 9 on the Richter scale.

There are pulling, pushing, and turning forces in action all around us.

Many words are used to describe the different forces in action around us. We use words such as magnetic force, electrostatic force, gravitational force, and squeezing, stretching, and bending. However, this range of words serves to describe just three different forces: pushing, pulling, and turning.

DID YOU KNOW?

The spectacular aurora borealis, or northern lights, is an ever-changing pattern of white or multicolored lights. It is caused by particles in the atmosphere, which are attracted toward the earth's magnetic poles. In the Southern Hemisphere there is a similar display, called the aurora australis.

4. Mark the spot your friend chooses with a cross and see how close to the magnet it is.

5. Now ask your friend to hide two magnets, and you try hunting them. This can be much harder!

ELECTROSTATIC FORCE

When you comb your hair, you often see individual hairs stand on end and move toward the comb: there seems to be a force attracting the hairs toward it. This is called electrostatic force, and it is an example of what static electricity can do. Electrostatic force makes dust cling to a television screen and drags ink powder onto the paper in a photocopier. When you take off a nylon sweater in the dark, the sparks you see are caused by static electricity.

Electrostatic force is produced when you rub two materials, such as a plastic balloon and a nylon sweater, together. The force occurs between materials that carry what is called an

The flashes of lightning you see during a thunderstorm are huge sparks caused by static electricity.

electric charge. The act of rubbing knocks electrons—subatomic particles that carry a negative charge—off the sweater, and they stick to the atoms of the balloon. The atoms of the sweater are left with a positive charge. As with the poles of magnets, there is a law of physics that says "opposite charges attract"; therefore, the negatively charged balloon sticks to the positively charged sweater. The law also says that "like charges repel": so, if two negatively charged balloons are brought close together, the electrostatic force pushes them apart.

SILVER DANCERS

MATERIALS
- an old (not valuable!) vinyl LP record
- a plastic or glass bowl
- silver balls used for decorating cakes
- a sharp pencil
- a dry cloth

1. Rub the record several times with the cloth, using a circular motion. This puts a negative charge on the record.

2. Carefully place the record over the bowl and put twelve silver balls on the surface. They will roll around for a few seconds and then stop.

3. Move the point of the pencil toward one of the balls. What happens to the ball?

WATER MAGIC

MATERIALS
- a copper rod
- a pencil
- a plastic ruler
- a wooden ruler or dowel rod
- a steel ruler
- a sweater
- a water faucet

1. Rub the plastic ruler against the sweater. After rubbing several times, the ruler will carry a negative charge.

2. Hold the ruler near a gentle stream of water. What happens, and why? Don't let the ruler get wet, or the effect will disappear.

3. Try the experiment again, using the other materials in turn. Note the effect that each one has on the stream of water.

MEASURING FORCES

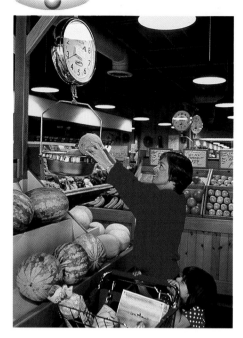

Forces are measured in units called newtons, named after Isaac Newton. If you hold a 2.2 lb. (1 kg) bag of sugar in your hand, gravity is pulling down on the bag with a force of nearly 10 newtons, or 10 N for short. If your mass is 110 lb. (50 kg), the earth is pulling on you with a force of 500 N, which is how scientists describe your weight. Confusingly, when you weigh things in stores, the weighing scales are usually marked in pounds or kilograms—the units of mass. It is easy to make the mistake of calling that measurement "weight."

Instruments used to measure forces are called forcemeters; if they are marked in newtons, they are called newtonmeters. The weighing scales in the supermarket or your bathroom scales are fairly inaccurate forcemeters, but most of them work in the same way as scientific newtonmeters, that is by either stretching or compressing (squeezing) a spring.

Supermarket weighing scales measure mass, not weight. The more mass an object has, the more strongly it is pulled toward the earth by gravity.

MAKE A FORCEMETER

1. Cut out a strip of cardboard and stick it or tack it along one edge of the wooden board.

2. Hammer the nail into the board, toward one end. Loop a rubber band around the nail and stand the board upright. With the pencil, draw a line on the cardboard opposite the lowest point of the rubber band.

MATERIALS
- a wooden board 12 in. x 6 in. (30 cm x 15 cm)
- rubber bands and springs of various sizes
- a ruler and a pencil
- stiff cardboard
- a small nail
- a hammer
- weighing scales marked in ounces and pounds (grams and kilograms)
- a plastic bag
- flour or rice
- thread
- scissors
- glue or thumbtacks

3. Weigh out 3.5 oz. (100 g) of flour or rice into the plastic bag and tie a length of thread around the neck of the bag to seal it.

4. Tie the thread to the bottom of the rubber band and, with the board upright, mark the cardboard opposite the new lowest point of the rubber band. Next to this point on the cardboard, write "1 N." (Remember: a mass of 2.2 lb. [1 kg] has a weight of 10 N on earth.)

WARNING!

● Be careful when using the hammer and nail.

5. Repeat steps **3** and **4** with bags weighing 7 oz. (200 g), 10.5 oz. (300 g), and so on, to make a force scale that can measure up to 10 N. The rubber band force measurer is accurate only when the distances between each mark on the scale are the same. By looking at the marks on your scale, you should be able to tell the smallest and largest forces your rubber band can measure.

6. Find five objects that you think your force measurer can weigh. Arrange them in order of weight by holding them in your hands. Now record the weights of the objects by hanging them from the thread on the rubber band. Was the order you guessed correct?

7. Experiment with other rubber bands and springs as force measurers. Which are more accurate at weighing, springs or rubber bands?

13

RESISTANCE

Have you seen the trick in which a magician quickly pulls a cloth from beneath a number of items on a table without breaking anything? Everything stays on the table in more or less the same position as before the trick. The reason for this is that all objects will resist a force trying to move them. This "unwillingness" to move is called inertia. The force needed to overcome the inertia of an object depends on the mass of the object. The objects laid on the table have sufficient inertia to resist the force of the moving tablecloth.

Inertia also keeps objects moving. Once launched into space, a spacecraft will travel forever until a force acts upon it. For the same reason, a moving object will resist any force that might alter the speed at which it is going or change its direction. Newton discovered this, and it became the first of his three laws of motion.

Resistance to movement comes not only from the inertia of the object itself, but also from whatever surface it is moving over. A ball rolling across grass will soon slow down and stop because of the resistance of the grass to the ball. The rougher the surface, the greater this force of resistance, or friction.

Skiers often use wax to reduce the friction between the snow and their skis; this helps them travel faster.

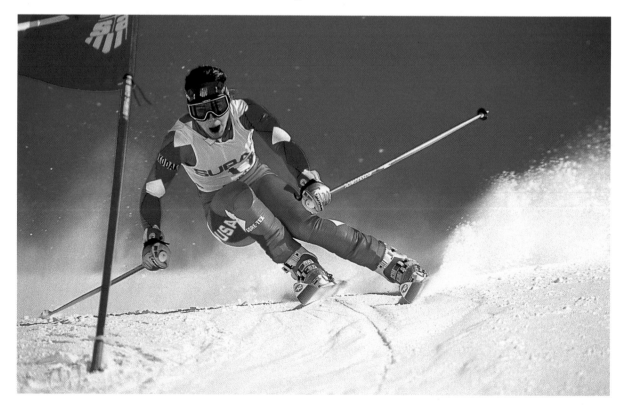

When objects must move quickly, friction can be a nuisance. For example, the moving parts of a car engine change a lot of energy into wasteful heat when they rub against each other. Oil is added to the engine to reduce the friction between its moving parts. But friction can also save lives. The force between the tread of a car's tires and the road slows the car down. In wet or icy conditions, the friction force is reduced and tires lose their grip.

SLIP AND GRIP

1. Draw a line across the board about 12 in. (30 cm) from one end and hammer the nails into the board, one at each end of the line. The nails will stop the test materials from slipping down the ramp.

2. Place a shoe on the board, making the toe of the shoe level with the line. Raise this end of the board until the shoe just starts to slide. At this point, the force of gravity is slightly greater than the friction force between the ramp and the shoe (the inertia of the shoe is small enough to ignore). Keeping the ramp at this angle, make a note of the height of the end of the board.

3. Repeat the test, placing the shoe on each of the different friction test materials in turn. Draw a bar chart on the graph paper to show the different ramp heights. What effect do the different materials have on the size of the friction force?

4. How does the material used to make the soles of the shoes, or the pattern on the soles, affect the friction force? Use the range of shoes you have collected to investigate these questions.

SLIPPERY SHAPES

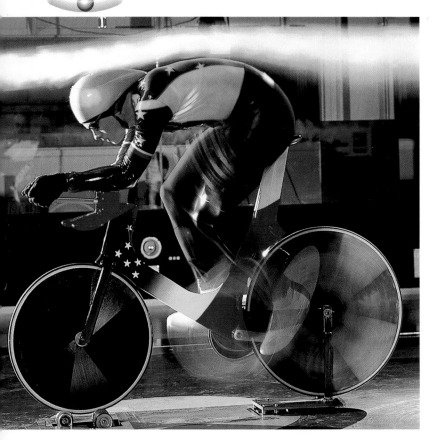

By testing models in a wind tunnel, designers can find the best shapes to reduce drag.

Motorcycles and cars, especially those used for racing, have shiny, rounded surfaces. This design makes the air flow smoothly over the vehicle and reduces drag. Motorcycle riders also have to make themselves as streamlined as possible by wearing skintight clothing and rounded crash helmets.

Water produces more drag than air. Designing a ship's hull is a complicated task, because the streamlined shapes that would increase its speed might also make it unstable. Ships need fins to make them stable, but these tend to increase drag. In ship-building the calculations are so precise that designers often use computers to help them find the best shape.

The force of friction not only resists movement over solid surfaces, but also occurs when objects move through fluids—liquids and gases. This type of friction is called drag.

Drag is sometimes useful, and sometimes not. Parachutists depend on the drag between the air and their parachutes to land safely. But people who design machines to move through air or water are usually very eager to keep drag forces as small as possible. That is because the more slippery, or streamlined, a vehicle's shape, the faster or farther it will travel on a given amount of fuel.

DID YOU KNOW?

Even trucks are streamlined! Their cabs are fitted with plastic scoops and deflectors to reduce the amount of fuel the trucks use. The deflectors do this by forcing the air to pass smoothly over the top or around the sides of the truck, thus reducing drag.

SHIPSHAPE

1. Place the gutter on a level table or other surface where the end of the gutter overhangs a drop of at least 3 ft. (1 m). Place the bricks or books on either side of the gutter to support it.

2. File a small groove in the middle of the overhanging end-stop. Carefully pour water into the gutter until it is three-quarters full.

3. Cut 8 ft. (2.4 m) of thread or line and tie one end to the bag of sand or rice. Attach the other end to the hook on one of the boat shapes.

4. Place one of the boat shapes in the water and slide the line through the groove letting the bag hang down. Hold the boat at the far end of the gutter and let it go. Start the clock and record the time it takes the boat to reach the end of the gutter.

5. Repeat the test for all the shapes. You should do each one more than once and figure out the average time for each one. Which shape has the most drag? Which is most streamlined?

MATERIALS

- a 6-ft. (2-m) length of rain gutter fitted with watertight end-stops
- a stopwatch
- a round file.
- a small plastic bag of rice or sand to act as a weight
- hull shapes cut from a piece of pine and fitted with small screw-in eyelets or cup hooks. The hulls should be shaped as differently as possible.
- 2 bricks or large books
- nylon thread or fishing line

17

FLIGHT

To get any object off the ground and keep it moving through the air, there are four forces to consider. These are *weight* and *drag,* which slow the object down, and *thrust* and *lift,* which tend to speed it up.

Most modern aircraft fly by using jet propulsion. The engines of a jet aircraft suck in air at the front. They compress, or squeeze, the air so that it gets very hot and they burn fuel in it. The burning mixture expands rapidly and rushes out of the rear of the engines, producing a huge thrust force.

Lift is a force produced when air moves over a surface, such as a wing or a propeller. The faster the aircraft flies, the greater the difference between the speed of the air flowing above and below the wing—and the greater the lift.

HIGH FLYERS

1. Cut out the wing, rudder, and tailplane shapes from the cardboard or balsa wood. Cut two 8-in. (20-cm) lengths and two 1.25 in. (3-cm) lengths of balsa wood and glue them together to make a frame for the fuselage of the plane.

2. Use a thin drill or bradawl to make a hole in each end of the wooden frame. Straighten the paper clips and thread the first through one end of the frame. Bend the end of the wire on the inside of the frame to make a hook.

3. On the outside of the frame, thread the bead and the propeller onto the wire and bend the wire to secure them. Make sure the propeller can spin easily.

MATERIALS

- a sheet of thin cardboard or balsa wood
- 20 in. (50 cm) of .4 in. (1 cm) square-section balsa wood
- a model propeller
- a large rubber band
- model glue
- 2 large paper clips
- a round bead
- a craft knife
- a drill or bradawl
- modeling clay

WARNING!

- Be careful when using the craft knife.

An aircraft's wing (right) is shaped to achieve lift.

Lift

Drag

Weight

Thrust

Air flows faster over the wing

Difference in air flow produces lift

Air flows slower below the wing

To keep an aircraft in flight (left), the forces of weight and drag are opposed by the forces of thrust and lift.

4. Thread the other paper clip through the hole in the opposite end of the frame and bend the end of the wire inside the frame to make a hook. Bend the other end of the wire so that it cannot easily be pulled through.

5. Attach the rubber band between the two hooks so that it is slightly taut. Glue the wings, rudder, and tailplane onto the frame.

6. Rest the model on a finger placed under the point where the wings are attached. If the plane does not stay level, add a small piece of modeling clay to the nose or the tail to make it balance.

7. Wind up the propeller until the rubber band is tight and, holding the plane just behind the wings, gently launch it into the air. How well does it fly?

8. Cut out some rectangles of cardboard about 2.5 x .75 in. (6 x 2 cm) and glue them along the rear edges of the wings, rudder, or tailplane to make flaps. Check that your plane still balances, adding modeling clay if necessary. How is its flight affected when you bend the flaps?

19

SURFACE TENSION

Surface tension is a pulling force. Liquids, such as falling rain and water dripping from a tap, are pulled into round drops by surface tension. The effect of the force is to try to pull the surface in toward the center of the drop. It seems to give the surface of the liquid a stretchable "skin," like a balloon. If you fill a glass with water very carefully to the brim, you can actually put in slightly more than the glass can hold. This is because surface tension pulls on the ultra-microscopic water molecules, keeping them in place and forming a mound of water, called a meniscus.

Again, if you carefully lay a paper clip on the surface, you will be able to see the "dent" that the clip makes on the water. It is only by weakening the links that hold the water molecules together that the surface tension can be broken; then the water will spread out, and the paper clip will sink. So, in order to wet a greasy object, such as a dinner plate, the water's skin must first be broken; soap and detergent achieve this by reducing the attraction between the water molecules.

However, soap does not destroy surface tension completely. A soap bubble is an amount of gas enclosed in an elastic soapy "skin."

Surface tension is a force that pulls bubbles and drops of water into a round shape.

If you blow a bubble by using a wire or plastic loop and stop blowing when the bubble is half-formed, it will shrink very rapidly and blow its air back at you! Surface tension is always trying to make bubbles smaller.

SURFACE TENSION BOAT

1. First wash your hands! Any grease on them will keep the boat from moving.

2. Trace the outline of the boat below onto the sheet of cardboard.

Cut   Cut

3. Cut along the solid lines and then fold the cardboard along the dotted lines, starting with the sides.

4. Fold back the cardboard at the front and rear of the boat. Glue the flaps where the front and sides overlap.

5. Cut out the two diamond shapes and wedge two small pieces of soap into the slits.

6. Half fill the dishpan with cold water and carefully place the boat on the surface. As the soap dissolves, it reduces the surface tension behind the boat and the greater surface tension force at the front pulls it forward.

UNDER PRESSURE

In science, pressure means how "spread out" a force is. People make use of pressure in many situations. You can't push your thumb into a wooden board, for example, but you can push a thumbtack into it. You can do this because the force of your thumb pushing on the head of the thumbtack is concentrated on a very small area under the point.

To determine the pressure under a force, you need to know two things: the size of the force, measured in newtons, and the area under the force. This can be written down as:

pressure = size of force ÷ by the area under the force

So, if a person weighing 600 newtons puts on a pair of skis that cover an area of 6,000 sq. cm (930 sq. in.), the pressure on the snow beneath the skier will be:

$600 \div 6,000 = 0.1$ newtons per square centimeter, or 0.1 N per sq. cm

When the skier takes off the skis, the area under her feet in normal shoes is only 600 square centimeters. This time the pressure will be:

$600 \div 600 = 1$ N per sq. cm

The pressure beneath the skier's feet is *ten times* greater now than it was when she had skis on. No wonder you sink into soft snow if you aren't wearing skis!

Everything that has weight exerts pressure. Water has pressure—the deeper you swim, the greater the water pressure. The air has pressure, too. In fact, the pressure of the atmosphere at ground level—about 10 N per sq. cm—would crush you if it were not for the pressure of the gas and liquid inside your body, which balances the air pressure on the outside.

Pressurized air is used in this car airbag to keep the driver safe in a collision.

Changes in "atmospheric pressure" (as the pressure of the air is called) are of great importance to pilots and weather forecasters. The higher you go, the lower the pressure. Aircraft altitude meters work by measuring the air pressure, while forecasters know that changes in air pressure can have dramatic effects on our weather. Many of us have devices called barometers in our homes; these predict changes in the weather by detecting small variations in atmospheric pressure and giving a reading on a dial.

SIMPLE BAROMETER

MATERIALS
- a drinking glass or tumbler
- a balloon
- a rubber band
- a drinking straw
- tape
- scissors
- a strip of poster board 8 in. x 2 in. (20 cm x 5 cm)
- a wooden base
- a pencil

1. Cut out a piece of balloon slightly larger than the open end of the tumbler. Stretch the balloon over the tumbler and secure it with a rubber band. Cut one end of the straw to make a point. Tape the other end of the straw to the stretched top of the balloon.

2. Fold the strip of poster board about 2 in. (5 cm) from the end to make a right angle, and tape it to one end of the wooden base so that the strip stands up.

3. Stand the glass at the other end of the base so that the pointed end of the straw lines up with the poster board strip. Place the barometer in a part of the house where the temperature stays the same all the time.

4. On the poster board strip, mark the level of the straw each day for one week to record changes in air pressure. A rising straw indicates an increase in atmospheric pressure, which usually means that good weather is on the way. How accurate is your barometer?

WATER PRESSURE

If you squeeze a gas, it becomes compressed. If you squeeze a bicycle pump with your finger over the end, you will find that the plunger still goes in a long way because the molecules making up the air are far enough apart to be pushed closer together. But if you were to fill the pump with water instead of air, you would find that the plunger hardly moves at all. Water molecules have very little space between them, so they cannot easily be compressed.

When you push on a liquid in a pipe, it is like pushing on a solid rod. Because liquids cannot be compressed, the force acting on them at one end of the pipe is passed on all the way to the other end. When a system of pipes containing a liquid is used to carry a force from one place to another, it is called a hydraulic system. "Hydraulic" means "having to do with water."

Hydraulic systems are very common. They are used to make car brakes work, for example, and to lift the buckets on mechanical diggers. The hydraulic systems in these machines do not use water—they use a special oil, contained in pipes that link two or more cylinders. Each cylinder has a piston that fits tightly into the end and moves up and down when the oil pushes or pulls against it.

The law of hydraulics says that if you exert a particular pressure over a large area, you produce a greater force than if you exert the same pressure over a small area. So, to stop a car, the driver pushes on the brake pedal which presses against a small piston inside a "master" cylinder of brake fluid. The fluid passes the force on through pipes to the brakes, where larger pistons, inside "slave" cylinders, produce a larger force on the brake shoes or pads. These push against the wheels and slow the car down.

Hydraulic power is used to lift heavy loads.

WEIGHT LIFTER

1. Blow up the balloon and let the air out several times so that it is stretched. Pull the end of the balloon over one end of the plastic pipe and seal the join with tape.

2. Cut the top off the plastic bottle and cut a hole in the side, near the base. Push the balloon on the end of the pipe through the hole.

3. Tape the funnel to the other end of the tube.

4. Place the can on top of the balloon in the bottle, and put the book or brick on top of the can.

DID YOU KNOW?

The five arms of a starfish are covered with flexible, hollow "tube feet" filled with water. The starfish can pump water in and out of these feet so that they straighten or bend. In this way, the starfish creeps across the seabed, using hydraulic power.

5. Keeping the funnel higher than the book or the brick, start pouring water into the funnel. Watch the balloon begin to swell and lift the can and the weight on top. How high can you lift the weight by using water power?

FLOATING AND SINKING

When you get into the bathtub, you may notice that the water level rises. By getting into the tub, you push some of the water out of the way. This is called *displacement*. If you could measure the volume of the water you have displaced, you would find that it is the same as the volume of your body. If you dangle a stone in water, it weighs less than if you weigh it out of water. Where has the "missing" weight gone?

There is a force that supports objects in water and in other fluids, such as a balloon in air. The force is *upthrust*. The deeper you go, whether into the ocean depths or to the "bottom" of the atmosphere (sea level), the greater the pressure. Upthrust is produced because the pressure of a fluid is greater at the bottom of an object than it is at the top, so the object is pushed upward. The upthrust force is equal to the weight of the fluid that the object displaces.

For an object to float in water or in air, it must generate at least as much upthrust as its own weight. For example, a ship must displace a volume of water that weighs more than itself. Ships are usually made of steel, so they must have hollow shapes to displace as much water as possible. If a ship is overloaded, its weight will be greater

Balloons float because the upthrust force on them from the air is greater than their own weight.

than the upthrust force, and it will sink. This is why there are markings, called Plimsoll lines, on the sides of ships; these show the lowest level at which it is safe for a ship to float.

DID YOU KNOW?

When a submarine needs to dive, it takes in water into special tanks. The water increases the weight of the submarine, so it is no longer supported by upthrust, and it sinks. When the submarine needs to rise to the surface again, water is pumped out of the tanks.

FLOATING CARGO

1. Cut three rectangular sheets of foil, each measuring 8 in. x 6 in. (20 cm x 15 cm). You are going to construct three boat hulls from these sheets.

2. Take the first sheet of foil and fold up each side .5 in. (1.3 cm). Bend each corner at right angles and tape it to make a watertight seal. You now have a shallow foil "hull" that you can load with cargo.

3. Repeat step **2** with the other sheets of foil, but fold up each side of the second sheet 1 in. (2.5 cm) and the third 1.5 in. (3.8 cm). You will then have three boat shapes with the same mass, but they will displace different amounts of water. This will make the floating test fair.

4. Half fill the bowl with water and place the first boat on the surface. Carefully put the first weight into the center of the hull and keep adding weights, one at a time, to all parts of the boat until it sinks. Write down the number of weights the boat can support.

5. Repeat the test for the other foil boats. Measure the area of the boats that is in contact with the water (by multiplying the length by the width). What is the link between the number of weights that can be supported by a boat and the area of the base of each hull?

MATERIALS

- a dishpan
- water
- aluminum foil
- a ruler
- 20 or so objects of similar weight, such as coins of the same value, large nails, or children's building blocks
- tape
- scissors

MAKING TASKS EASIER

We use machines to make tasks easier. Machines magnify the forces we exert with our muscles so that we can move objects that would otherwise be too heavy for us. Most of the machines we use are operated by *levers* or *pulleys*. These are useful where a small force moving over a great distance is needed to move a much heavier load over a short distance.

Levers are found in tools as varied as scissors, screwdrivers, wheelbarrows,

Types of levers

Load · Effort · Fulcrum

Effort · Load · Fulcrum

Effort · Load · Fulcrum

CATAPULT

1. Drill holes 1 in. (3 cm) apart along the lengths of square-section wood. The holes in the two uprights (the shorter lengths) should line up and be big enough to fit the dowel.

2. Stand the uprights on the baseboard and nail them into position. Nail the Masonite triangles to the uprights and the baseboard for support.

3. Attach the plastic cup to one end of the long length of wood, using a thumbtack. Hold this length between the uprights and push the dowel rod through one set of the holes, if necessary securing it at each end with a thumbtack. The dowel is the fulcrum of the catapult lever.

WARNING!
- Ask an adult to help you with this project.
- Make sure you only test your catapult out-of-doors.

MATERIALS
- a plastic drinking cup
- 2 8-in. (20-cm) lengths and 1 12-in. (30-cm) length of .75-in. (2-cm) square-section wood
- a 12 in. x 5 in. (30 cm x 13 cm) wooden base
- 2 Masonite triangles, each side measuring 4 in. (10 cm)
- a 5-in. (13-cm) length of dowel and a hand drill with the same diameter
- 2 screw hooks
- a thick rubber band
- thumbtacks
- pieces of sponge
- watercolor paints
- a sheet of cardboard for the target
- finishing nails and a hammer

bottle openers, and weighing scales. There are three parts to any lever: the point where you exert a force, or effort; the point, or fulcrum, where the lever pivots; and the point where the load is applied. The task that a lever can do depends on the position of these three points in relation to each other.

If you wanted to lift a heavy bucket of sand to the top of a building, you would use a pulley. A pulley changes a downward pull on one end of a rope into an upward pull at the other end. With two pulleys instead of one, you can lift even more weight with the same effort. But you don't get something for nothing—the bucket will travel only half the distance that the pulleys travel!

Types of pulleys

Single pulley

Double pulley

(only half the effort needed to lift the same load)

Effort

Effort

Load

Load

4. Screw one hook into the other end of the long length of wood and screw the other hook into the baseboard. Attach the rubber band between the hooks.

5. Make a target with colored zones for different scores and tack it to a wall or fence, or lay it on the ground. Soak the sponges in the paint and place one in the plastic cup. This is the load part of the catapult lever.

6. Push down on the cup end of the catapult and see the rubber band stretch. This provides the effort part of the catapult lever. Let go, and see where the paint sponge lands. Adjust your aim in order to land your sponges on the target.

7. How does changing the distance between the fulcrum and the effort affect how far the sponge load travels? Alter the position of the dowel rod to find out.

BALANCING ACT

One of the simplest levers is a playground seesaw. With this, each child in turn provides the effort to lift the other child, who is the load. You may have noticed yourself how hard it is to lift a person on the other end of a seesaw if that person is heavier than you. The forces at each end are unbalanced. The only way to balance them is for the lighter child to sit farther away from the fulcrum than the heavier one. With the children in these positions, a scientist would say that the turning force of the lighter child is equal to the turning force of the heavier one.

When two forces are balanced, as they are when the seesaw is horizontal, the single point around which the opposing forces turn is called the center of gravity. Every object has a center of gravity; it is the point where the pulling force of gravity seems to be concentrated. For example, when a gymnast is performing an exercise, she knows that she must keep her center of gravity exactly over the narrow beam. If she doesn't, the turning forces on either side of the beam will become unbalanced and she will fall off!

The center of gravity of an object is determined by its shape and the position of most of its mass. A tall, thin object with most of its mass toward the top has a high center of gravity. It would take only a small amount of force to push it over. An object such as this is described as unstable. On the other hand, a short object with a wide base has a low center of gravity. It is much harder to push over. Scientifically, you would say it is more stable.

In order to balance, this gymnast must keep her center of gravity over the beam.

HIGH-WIRE ACT

1. Using the cardboard, draw, color, and cut out a clown figure with its arms outstretched, as shown in the photograph below.

2. Cut a small notch in the head of the clown and use modeling clay to attach a washer to each hand.

3. Stretch the string between the necks of the bottles and place the clown so that the string fits into the notch. The clown will balance because its center of gravity is between its hands, below the level of the string. Give one of the bottles a sharp tap and see the clown wobble to keep his balance!

4. Try cutting out other shapes that will balance, such as this parrot.

MATERIALS

- a sheet of stiff cardboard
- 2 metal washers
- colored pencils
- scissors
- 20 in. (50 cm) of thin string
- modeling clay
- 2 bottles of water

STRONG SHAPES

Some objects are stronger than you would expect. They owe their strength to two factors: the material they are made of, and their shape. For example, if you were to stab a potato very quickly with a drinking straw, the straw would go right through it! Although a straw is easy to bend, it is very hard to crush lengthwise. Cylinders, such as straws, are strong structures. A bicycle frame is made up of metal cylinders to give the bicycle strength and reduce weight. Even the bones in your own skeleton are tube-shaped.

Another shape used to strengthen structures, ranging from bicycles to bridges, is the triangle. A structure built of triangles cannot easily be twisted or collapsed. Any forces pushing down on such a building are supported by the many corners. The Eiffel Tower in Paris is made almost entirely of

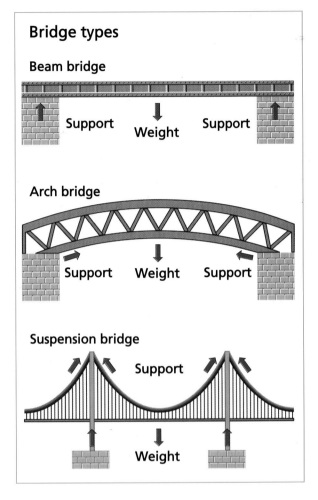

Bridge types

Beam bridge

Support   Weight   Support

Arch bridge

Support   Weight   Support

Suspension bridge

Support

Weight

BRIDGE THE GAP

1. Place the two books on a table and measure 12 in. (30 cm) between them. This is the distance you need to cross with your bridge.

2. Remembering what you have read about strong shapes, investigate ways of using the straws to build a bridge across the gap. Use only the smallest amounts of tape necessary to stick one bridge beam to another. The bridge mustn't obtain any strength from the tape you use.

MATERIALS
- 30 5-in. (12-cm) lengths cut from paper straws (NOT flexible straws)
- a ruler
- scissors
- tape
- two books of equal thickness

triangles—it even has a triangular shape itself.

The science of strong shapes is perhaps best shown in the design of bridges. A properly constructed bridge must support its own weight as well as the weight of the traffic crossing it. The simplest bridges are beam bridges; these consist of a single "span" (the distance between the bridge supports). But beam bridges cannot support their own weight beyond a certain length. Arch bridges are stronger because the arch spreads more of the weight onto the supports. Once steel and concrete became widely available, bridge builders were able to build much longer and stronger bridges, such as modern suspension bridges. These use extremely strong steel cables to link concrete towers at each end of the bridge, or on islands. The strong shape of suspension bridges allows them to resist the downward force of the traffic and the sideways force of high winds.

The Eiffel Tower is a strong, triangular structure with a low center of gravity.

3. Build two bridges so that you can compare them for strength. You should think about how you are going to test the strength of the bridges when you design and build them. Include in your designs a platform of some sort for loading the bridge with weights.

ON THE MOVE

How do you make something move? If the object is not too big, you can use your muscles to exert the force required. But objects with greater mass require bigger forces, and you may have to use a machine with an engine to start them moving. Other than your own muscle force, the force that produces the most movement is gravity, which pulls objects toward the earth.

What happens to a moving object when you stop pushing or pulling it? The ancient Greeks believed that when an arrow was fired into the air, it was the air itself that kept the arrow moving. They thought that, unless the air exerted its own force, the arrow

The energy for movement can come from many different sources.

would immediately fall to the ground when the bowstring stopped pushing it. Eventually the Greeks decided that the reason the arrow fell to earth was "natural motion," because the ground was its "natural" place.

It was not until the great Italian scientist Galileo began his studies of moving objects that anyone came up with a different idea. Galileo showed that once an object was moving, no extra force was needed to keep it moving. He said that an object stops moving when another force acts on it. As we have already seen, the force that acts against movement is friction. Only in deep space, away from the gravitational pull of any planet, can a rocket keep going without slowing down. Newton took Galileo's ideas further. He said not only can a force make an object move, but it can also change how fast it moves and the direction in which it is moving. Newton's first law of motion states that "an object will move only when a force acts on it, and a moving object will keep on moving at the same speed and in the same direction unless a force changes the object's speed or direction."

MAKING THINGS MOVE

1. It is best to do this project out-of-doors, on a hard surface. Set up the ramp on the stool and draw a line across the board where it rests on the stool. This will be the start line for the ramp tests.

2. Place a toy behind the line and let it run down the slope and across the floor. How far does it go? Repeat the test twice more and work out the average distance traveled (total distance traveled in three attempts divided by 3).

3. Using the nails, attach the spools about 6 in. (15 cm) apart on the square board. Stretch a large rubber band around the spools. You may need two rubber bands looped together. Pull back the rubber band to make a catapult and place a toy vehicle in it. Let go of the rubber band. How far does the vehicle go? Try the test several times and determine the average distance traveled.

4. Hold the toy vehicle steady on the floor with one hand. Give it a hard push and let go. How far does it go? Repeat as before to figure out the average distance traveled.

5. Try each way of making a vehicle move, using two other toys.

6. Use the graph paper and colored pencils to make a bar chart of your measurements. From what you have read about forces and motion, can you suggest why one car goes farther than the others?

SPEED

When people say the top speed of a certain car is 185 mph (300 km/h), they mean that the car would cover 185 mi. (300 km) if driven at that speed for one hour. Of course, cars are seldom driven that way. It is more usual to talk about the average speed over a distance; this evens out the different speeds along the way and takes into account other traffic or poor roads.

With its sleek coat and slim body, the streamlined cheetah is the world's fastest land animal.

If a car travels 60 mi. (100 km) in two hours, its average speed is figured out by dividing the distance by the time:

$$\text{average speed} = \frac{\text{distance traveled}}{\text{time taken}}$$
$$= \frac{60\ (100)}{2}$$
$$= 30\ \text{mph}\ (50\ \text{km/h})$$

Scientists usually measure speed in meters per second (m/s) rather than miles per hour or kilometers per hour, so 30 mph (50 km/h) would be written

RAMP RACERS

1. In a large, open space with an even surface, arrange some books to make a stack 4 in. (10 cm) tall. Lean the ramp against the books and mark a line across it where it touches the books.

2. Place your car behind the line and set your stopwatch to zero. Let the car go and immediately start the stopwatch. Time how long it takes for the car to roll down the ramp, cross the floor, and come to a halt.

MATERIALS
- toy cars
- a 3-ft. (1-m) wooden ramp
- books of assorted thicknesses
- a ruler
- a stopwatch
- a long measuring tape
- a pencil

as 13.9 m/s (50,000 meters divided by 60, and divided by 60 again). If you walk as fast as possible, you can probably walk at around 2 m/s and run at about 5 m/s. A champion sprinter can run a 100-meter race in 10 seconds, which is a speed of 10 m/s.

The chart below shows the top air, land, and sea speeds for some animals and machines, in meters per second.

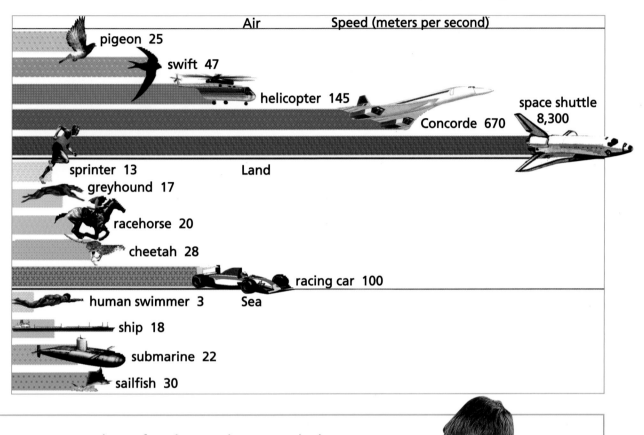

Air Speed (meters per second)

pigeon 25
swift 47
helicopter 145
Concorde 670
space shuttle 8,300

sprinter 13 **Land**
greyhound 17
racehorse 20
cheetah 28
racing car 100

human swimmer 3 **Sea**
ship 18
submarine 22
sailfish 30

3. Measure how far the car has traveled. You can now figure out its average speed. Do the test again and find the average speed for the two runs.

4. Repeat the test, using more books to make ramps of different heights, say 8 in. (20 cm) and 12 in. (30 cm). What effect does raising the height of the ramp have on the average speed of the car?

FASTER AND SLOWER

Formula 1 racing cars can accelerate from 0–90 mph (0–150 km/h) in about 3 seconds.

When you get into a car and it starts to move off, you can tell that it is going faster and faster. You feel pressed back into your seat. When the car reaches and maintains a certain speed, you no longer feel pressed back. It is the same whether you are traveling at 60 mph (100 km/h) or 120 mph (200 km/h). You experience the "pressed back" feeling only when you speed up— or accelerate to—a steady speed.

Acceleration describes any change in speed. You are accelerating if you speed up or if you slow down. Slowing down is sometimes called deceleration. Car manufacturers calculate the acceleration figures of their cars by knowing how long it takes to achieve a certain speed. A car that can accelerate from stationary (not moving) to 60 mph (100 km/h) in 10 seconds is accelerating at:

$$\frac{\text{change in speed}}{\text{time taken}} = \frac{60\ (100)}{10}$$

$$= \text{6 miles (10 km) per hour per second, or 6 mph/s (10 km/h/s)}$$

This means that at the end of every second of a 10-second test, the car is traveling 6 mph (10 km/h) faster than at the end of the second before. In the same way, when the car is slowing down, going from 60 mph (100 km/h) to stationary in 10 seconds, the deceleration is the same figure, but scientists might write a minus sign in front of the 6 mph/s (10 km/h/s) to show that it is slowing down.

DID YOU KNOW?

When jet fighters come in to land on an aircraft carrier, they decelerate so quickly that the pilots sometimes black out for a few seconds. The same thing can happen when a pilot ejects from an aircraft, but in this case the problem is caused by the enormous acceleration.

SPEEDY SPOTS

1. Cut off the top 2 in. (5 cm) of the detergent bottle and push a pin through the cap to make a small hole. Tape the cut section of the bottle to the rear of the toy. This is the reservoir.

2. Mix a few drops of food coloring with some glycerine in a jar and pour the mixture into the reservoir. Adjust the size of the hole in the cap so that the coloring drips at about five drops per second. Seal the hole with modeling clay.

3. Tape a strip of paper onto the wooden board and place one end of the board on a stack of books. Hold the toy at the top of the slope. Remove the modeling clay and let the toy roll down the slope.

4. Reseal the hole in the cap and allow the spots on the strip to dry. What do you notice about the distance between the spots? Why do you think this happened?

5. Repeat the test with the board at a steeper angle. What happens to the distance between the spots? How does the slope of the board affect the acceleration of the toy?

ACTION AND REACTION

What do rockets and runners have in common? The answer is that they both illustrate Isaac Newton's laws of motion. Take the launch of the space shuttle, for example. Before the engine fires, the shuttle is still: this illustrates the first law (that an object at rest will stay at rest until a force acts upon it). When the engine fires, the shuttle lifts off: this illustrates the second law, which says that "when a force acts on an object, the object changes its speed or direction in the same direction as the force that has been applied."

The space shuttle's launch demonstrates Newton's three laws of motion.

BALLOON ROCKETS

MATERIALS
- balloons of assorted shapes
- 15–30 ft. (5-10 m) of smooth string or strong thread
- drinking straws
- tape
- scissors
- thin cardboard

1. Thread the string through a drinking straw.

The rocket lifts off because there is a tremendous force on it, which comes from the burning gas streaming backward from the engines. This illustrates Newton's third law, which says that "for every force—or action—there is an equal force—or reaction—against it."

When you run, you may think it is your muscles that move you forward, but it is the reaction of the ground against the backward push of your feet that is pushing with just as much force. If the ground did not produce an equal reaction force, you would sink into the ground, as if it were water.

A simple test to illustrate Newton's third law is for you and a friend to put on roller skates and stand facing each other on a smooth surface. Put your hands together and push gently, staying as upright as you can. Instead of pushing your friend away, you both roll backward! If your friend is heavier than you, then you will roll back more than he or she does. If you are both the same weight, you will roll back the same distance.

2. Blow up the balloon and attach it with tape to the straw.

3. Keeping the string taut, release the balloon. The sudden release of air is jet propulsion. How far does the balloon travel?

4. Try the test with other balloon shapes. Do some balloons make better rockets than others?

5. Try adding triangles of cardboard as fins to stabilize the balloon in "flight."

COLLISIONS

When a moving ball collides with a moving bat, you would expect the ball to shoot off in a different direction and at a higher speed than before. You would also expect the bat to keep on moving in the same direction, but perhaps a little slower. What decides that the ball will move faster after the collision, and not the bat? The two important things to consider are the speed and the mass of the ball and the bat.

Scientists combine speed and mass in one idea, called momentum. If two objects are moving toward each other at the same speed, but one has a greater mass than the other, then it has more momentum. When the objects collide, the total momentum of the two objects, added together, is shared equally between them. If their masses stay the same as before, the lighter object will go faster after the collision, while the heavier object will go slower. This is one of the laws of science, and it is called the law of conservation of momentum (conservation means "to stay the same").

Every day, collisions occur that show what damage the law of conservation of momentum can do. These are road accidents and accidents that occur during sports and games when the players are not using protective clothing or equipment.

Football players wear special clothing to protect themselves while playing.

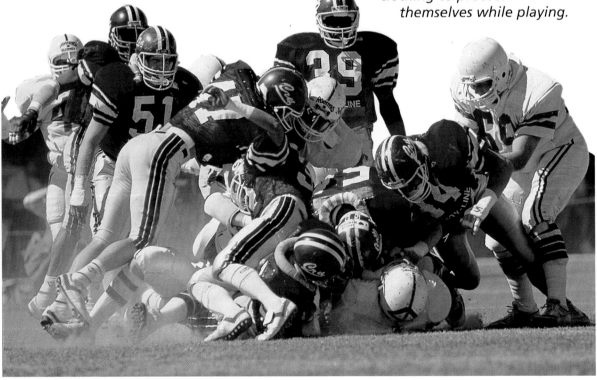

MINI POOL

MATERIALS

- a large sheet of shiny cardboard or bristol board
- 9 checkers (4 black, 4 white, and 1 other)
- scissors
- a ruler
- a felt-tipped pen
- colored labels
- a shoe box or empty cereal box, smaller all around than the shiny cardboard
- tape

1. With the scissors, score along each side of the sheet of cardboard, about 1 in. (2.5 cm) in from the edge. Cut a small square out of each corner so that the edges can be turned up and the corners taped. This is your pool table.

2. Cut a hole in each corner of the "table," big enough to let a checker fall through. Put the "table" on the empty box.

3. Mark a spot on one of the checkers, using the pen or a colored label and place it near the edge of the pool table. Use pieces of the label to number each set of checkers from 1–4. These are the point values of each checker. Place the eight numbered checkers in the center of the table.

4. With a friend, take a set of checkers each. Take turns knocking each other's checkers into a corner "pocket" by flicking the marked checker so that it strikes either a black or a white checker. Record the number of points, and take an extra turn whenever you "pocket" a checker.

ROUND AND ROUND

If you swing a bucket of water in a circle, the water will not spill out (as long as the bucket is moving fast enough!). That is because the water is pushing against the bucket as the bucket tries to travel in a straight line. Remember, Newton's first law says that a moving object will continue in a straight line unless acted upon by a force. (If you let go of the bucket, you would provide this force!) You have to pull on the handle of the bucket to

To keep the bike turning the corner, a racing motorcyclist has to lean into the corner; otherwise, he would travel straight ahead.

LOOP THE LOOP

1. Cut the sheet of cardboard into four or five strips, 20 in. x 2.5 in. (50 cm x 6 cm) each. Score two lines along the length of each strip, so that the edges can be folded up to make a U-shaped track about 1 in. (2.5 cm) wide. These are the sections that you will tape together to make your roller-coaster ride.

2. Make vertical cuts about every 1 in. (2.5 cm) along the sides of two of the track sections. Line up the cuts on one side with those on the opposite side.

3. Bend the tracks so that the cuts overlap. Tape across the cuts to shape each track into a semicircle. Depending on the stiffness of your cardboard and the closeness of the cuts, you may be able to make almost complete circles out of both sections of track.

4. Use tape to assemble the sections of track so that one end is raised much higher than the rest. Make sure that no tape is showing on the inside of the track to slow the marble down. The track should start with a straight section, lead into one or two loops, and finish with another straight section.

MATERIALS
- a large sheet of thin cardboard or poster board 20 in. (50 cm) square
- a ruler
- scissors
- tape
- marbles of different sizes

WARNING!
- Be careful when scoring the cardboard.

keep it moving in a circle. The force you exert on the bucket is called centripetal force. This force is constantly making the bucket change direction, turning in toward the center of the circle—you! The faster you swing the bucket, the greater is the centripetal force you need to exert to keep it moving.

People often confuse centripetal force with a force that seems to push things out from the center: this is called centrifugal force. In fact, centrifugal force does not exist—it is just the natural resistance, or inertia, of an object to changing its speed or direction.

5. Hold a marble at the top of the first section and let it go. Does it loop the loop? You may need to adjust the size of the loop or the height of the first section so that the marble gets to the end of the track. Which marbles loop the loop best: the heavier or the lighter ones? How can you make the marbles travel faster down the track?

GLOSSARY

Acceleration A change in speed or direction.

Atmospheric pressure Pressure exerted by the movement of gas molecules in the atmosphere.

Barometer A device for measuring air pressure.

Center of gravity The point at which the mass of an object seems to be concentrated.

Centripetal force The force that keeps a rotating object moving in a circle.

Conservation of momentum The principle that momentum is never lost. Momentum is calculated by multiplying the mass of an object by its speed. When two objects collide, the sum of their momentum after the collision is the same as the sum of their momentum before the collision.

Drag The tendency for air or a liquid to slow a moving object.

Force A push, pull, or turn. Something that changes the shape or motion of an object.

Friction The force that resists movement when one surface slides over another.

Fulcrum The point at which a lever pivots.

Gravity The force of attraction between two objects. The size of the force depends on the mass of the object.

Hydraulics The transfer of force through a liquid.

Inertia An object's resistance to movement or to a change in motion.

Lever A simple machine that reduces the effort needed to lift a load. A lever consists of a rigid beam turning around a fulcrum.

Mass The measure of an amount of matter. Wherever the measurement is made, an object's mass does not change.

Momentum see **Conservation of momentum**.

Newton The unit of force needed to accelerate a mass of 1 kg 1 meter per second

Pressure The force exerted over a particular area.

Speed The rate at which an object moves. Average speed is found by dividing the distance traveled by the time taken.

Surface tension A force that tends to pull the surface of a liquid into the smallest possible area, usually a sphere, like a raindrop.

Thrust The force that propels a rocket or an aircraft.

Weight A measure of the force of gravity acting on a mass.

BOOKS TO READ

Ardley, Neil. *The Science Book of Motion*. San Diego: Harcourt Brace, 1992.

Bardon, Keith. *Exploring Forces and Structures* (Exploring Science). Austin, TX: Raintree Steck-Vaughn, 1992.

Friedhoffer, Robert. *Force, Motion, and Energy* (Scientific Magic). Danbury, CT: Franklin Watts, 1992.

Gardner, Robert. *Forces and Machines* (Investigate and Discover). Parsippany, NJ: Silver Burdett Press, 1991.

Graham, Ian. *How Things Work*. New York: Facts on File, 1994.

Lafferty, Peter. *Force and Motion* (Eyewitness Science). New York: Dorling Kindersley, 1992.

Peacock, Graham. *Forces* (Science Activities). Austin, TX: Raintree Steck-Vaughn, 1994.

Sauvain, Philip. *Motion* (The Way It Works). Parsippany, NJ: Silver Burdett Press, 1992.

ANSWERS TO QUESTIONS

Answers to questions posed in the projects.

Pages 6–7 Both balls hit the clay at the same time. Weight does not affect the speed of the balls. The heavier ball will have made a deeper/wider dent. The size of an object does not affect the speed at which it falls, provided that the object's weight is much greater than the force of air resistance.

Pages 10–11 Silver Dancers: The ball will jump away to another groove on the disk. Water Magic: The water stream will bend toward the ruler, which attracts the positive charge on the water molecules.

Pages 12–13 Springs are generally more accurate than rubber bands; they will be more reliable over several measurements.

Pages 14–15 Shiny, smooth materials, such as plastic or leather, have a low friction force. Rough, "sticky" materials, such as rubber and carpet, have a high friction force. On the soles of the shoes, a zigzag pattern of cuts gives more friction force.

Pages 16–17 A square or rectangular hull has most drag, while a pointed, triangular shape is most streamlined.

Pages 18–19 Bending the flaps will make the plane swoop up or down. Bending the rudder will turn it left or right.

Pages 26–27 The greater the area of the base of the boat, the more weights it will support.

Pages 28–29 The greater the distance between the fulcrum and the effort, the farther the sponge load travels.

Pages 34–35 One car will go farther than another if there is less friction between the wheels and the surface (the board or the floor), or if it has a more streamlined shape, or if it is lighter.

Pages 36–37 The steeper the ramp, the greater the average speed of the cars.

Pages 38–39 The distance between the ink spots increases because the car is moving farther in the time between each drop. With the board at a steeper angle, the distance between the spots increases even more because the car accelerates faster as the slope is made steeper.

Pages 44–45 Within broad limits, the lighter (smaller) marbles will loop the loop better than heavier (larger) marbles. Raise the end of the track to increase the speed of the marbles, or flick them with a finger.

INDEX